TWEETABLE
WILLIAM SHAKESPEARE

Infotainment Press

TWEETABLE
WILLIAM
SHAKESPEARE

QUIPS, QUOTES & OTHER ONE-LINERS

There's place and means for every man alive.

Methought I heard a voice cry, Sleep no more!
Macbeth does murder sleep! The innocent sleep.

Thou art the ruins of the noblest man that ever lived in
the tide of times.

There have been many great men that have flattered
the people who ne'er loved them.

O tiger's heart wrapp'd in a woman's hide!

Virtue is choked with foul ambition.

Rosencrantz and Guildenstern are dead.

You must wear your rue with a difference. There's
a daisy. I would give you some violets, but they
withered all when my father died.

Had it pleas'd heaven to try me with affliction . . .
I should have found in some place of my soul
a drop of patience.

The little foolery that wise men have makes
a great show.

A man can die but once.

I would fain die a dry death.

The fashion of the world is to avoid cost, and you encounter it.

Ambition, the soldier's virtue, rather makes choice of loss, than gain which darkens him.

Let's talk of graves, of worms, and epitaphs. Make dust our paper, and with rainy eyes write sorrow on the bosom of the earth.

I can sing, and speak to him in many sorts of music.

*O*ur purses shall be proud, our garments poor; for 'tis the mind that makes the body rich.

*T*o die, to sleep; to sleep, perchance to dream— ay, there's the rub.

*H*ow oft the sight of means to do ill deeds makes ill deeds done!

*A*nd with some sweet oblivious antidote cleanse the stuff'd bosom of that perilous stuff which weighs upon the heart?

Our jovial star reigned at his birth.

How far your eyes may pierce, I cannot tell; striving to better, oft we mar what's well.

Speak of me as I am; nothing extenuate, nor set down aught in malice.

My mistress' eyes are nothing like the sun; coral is far more red than her lips' red.

Wisely, and slow. They stumble that run fast.

How much more doth beauty beauteous seem by that sweet ornament which truth doth give!

How oft when men are at the point of death have they been merry!

Et tu, Brute!

Against love's fire fear's frost hath dissolution.

However do we praise ourselves, our fancies are more giddy and uniform, more longing, wavering, sooner lost and worn, than women's are.

Though music oft hath such a charm to make bad good, and good provoke to harm.

Virtue itself scapes not calumnious strokes.

He that dies pays all debts.

Tell me where is Fancy bred, or in the heart, or in the head.

Trifles light as air are to the jealous confirmations strong as proofs of holy writ.

*H*e hath bore me on his back a thousand times, and now—how abhorred in my imagination it is.

*S*weet mercy is nobility's true badge.

O! for a muse of fire, that would ascend the brightest heaven of invention.

*N*or Mars his sword nor wars quick fire shall burn the living record of your memory.

*W*hat seest thou else in the dark backward and abysm of time?

How all occasions do inform against me,
and spur my dull revenge.

These pretty pleasures might me move to live with thee
and be thy love.

Absence from those we love is self from self—a deadly
banishment.

I love to hear her speak, yet well I know that music hath
a far more pleasing sound.

They say, best men are molded out of faults, and,
for the most, become much more the better
for being a little bad.

It is not in the stars to hold our destiny
but in ourselves.

I must be cruel only to be kind; thus bad begins, and worse remains behind.

Where be your gibes now, your gambols, your songs, your flashes of merriment, that were wont to set the table on a roar?

I shall the effect of this good lesson keep as watchman to my heart.

While you live tell truth and shame the devil.

How quickly nature falls into revolt when gold becomes her object!

Full fathom five thy father lies;
of his bones are coral made.

Is this a dagger which I see before me, the handle toward
my hand? Come, let me clutch thee.

A woman mov'd is like a fountain troubled, muddy, ill-
seeming, thick, bereft of beauty.

My soul is in the sky.

For Brutus is an honourable man; so are they all, all
honourable men.

Do as adversaries do in law, strive mightily, but eat and drink as friends.

Perseverance . . . keeps honor bright: to have done, is to hang quite out of fashion, like a rusty nail in monumental mockery.

I never knew so young a body with so old a head.

I do know of these that only are reputed wise for saying nothing.

This is the short and the long of it.

O, then, what graces in my love do dwell, that he hath turn'd a heaven unto hell!

*H*ow use doth breed a habit in a man.

*G*ive me my Romeo; and, when I shall die, take him and cut him out in little stars.

*Y*ou all did see, that on the Lupercal I thrice presented him a kingly crown, which he did thrice refuse. Was this ambition?

*B*eauty provoketh thieves sooner than gold.

Beware of entrance to a quarrel; but being in, bear't that the opposed may beware of thee.

O, that this too solid flesh would melt, thaw and resolve itself into a dew!

Thank me no thankings nor proud me no prouds.

O jest unseen, inscrutable, invisible, as a nose on a man's face, or a weathercock on a steeple.

In peace there's nothing so becomes a man as modest stillness and humility.

And oft, my jealousy shapes faults that are not.

Love lacked a dwelling, and made him her place; and when in his fair parts she did abide, she was lodged and newly deified.

Nothing can come of nothing.

I have wedded her, not bedded her; and sworn to make the "not" eternal.

Show me a mistress that is passing fair, what doth her beauty serve but as a note where I may read who pass'd that passing fair?

The choice and master spirits of this age.

My bounty is as boundless as the sea, my love as deep; the more I give to thee, the more I have, for both are infinite.

We are time's subjects, and time bids be gone.

Though it be honest, it is never good to bring bad news.

Thus conscience does make cowards of us all.

Costly thy habit as thy purse can buy, But not express'd in fancy; rich, not gaudy; for the apparel oft proclaims the man.

O, it is excellent to have a giant's strength; but it is tyrannous to use it like a giant.

There's many a man has more hair than wit.

Pray you now, forget and forgive.

All the world's a stage, and all the men and women merely players.

Farewell, my sister, fare thee well. The elements
be kind to thee, and make thy spirits all of comfort:
fare thee well.

How poor are they who have not patience!
What wound did ever heal but by degrees.

Thy wish was father . . . to that thought.

The empty vessel makes the loudest sound.

Expectation is the root of all heartache.

But O, how bitter a thing it is to look into happiness through another man's eyes.

Are you sure that we are awake? It seems to me that yet we sleep, we dream.

Present mirth hath present laughter; what's to come is still unsure.

I, thus neglecting worldly ends, all dedicated to closeness and the bettering of my mind.

Wrest once the law to your authority— to do a great right, do a little wrong.

Do not cast away an honest man
for a villain's accusation.

My meaning in saying he is a good man, is to have you understand me that he is sufficient.

Who is here so base, that would be a bondman? If any, speak, for him have I offended.

My reason, the physician to my love, angry that his prescriptions are not kept, hath left me.

This day is called the feast of Crispian. He that outlives this day and comes safe home will stand a-tiptoe when this day is named.

Oh, that way madness lies; let me shun that.

Virtue and genuine graces in themselves speak what no words can utter.

The devil hath power to assume a pleasing shape.

My only love sprung from my only hate. Too early seen unknown, and known too late.

For I have neither wit, nor words, nor worth, action, nor utterance, nor the power of speech to stir men's blood. I only speak right on.

My crown is called content, a crown that seldom kings enjoy.

The rest is silence.

Rough winds do shake the darling buds of May, and summer's lease hath all too short a date.

Truth is truth to the end of reckoning.

For thy sweet love remember'd such wealth brings that then I scorn to change my state with kings.

The ancient saying is no heresy, hanging and wiving goes by destiny.

I am not in the giving vein today.

*L*et ill tidings tell themselves when they be felt.

*I*t is twice blest: it blesseth him that gives and him that takes.

*Y*ou take my life when you do take the means whereby I live.

*F*or in the very torrent, tempest, and whirlwind of passion, you must acquire and beget a temperance that may give it smoothness.

The play, I remember, pleased not the million, 'twas caviare to the general.

How like a winter hath my absence been from thee, the pleasure of the fleeting year!

Lawless are they that make their wills their law.

Farewell! Thou art too dear for my possessing.

Thou art the Mars of malcontents.

The lunatic, the lover, and the poet, are of imagination all compact.

Words without thoughts never to heaven go.

Forbear to judge, for we are sinners all.

Things without all remedy should be without regard: what's done is done.

Now get you to my lady's chamber, and tell her, let her paint an inch thick, to this favour she must come.

*I*t is too rash, too unadvis'd, too sudden.

*N*ow my love is thaw'd; which, like a waxen image
'gainst a fire, bears no impression of the thing it was.

*M*y tables. Meet it is I set it down That one may smile,
and smile, and be a villain.

*D*eny thy father and refuse thy name. Or if thou
wilt not, be but sworn my love and I'll no longer
be a Capulet.

*T*each not thy lip such scorn, for it was made for
kissing, lady, not for such contempt.

Can one desire too much of a good thing?

She cannot love, nor take no shape nor project or affection, she is so self-endeared.

No ceremony that to great ones 'longs, not the king's crown . . . nor the judge's robe, become them with one half so good a grace as mercy does.

The iron tongue of midnight hath told twelve; lovers to bed; 'tis almost fairy time.

Suspicion always haunts the guilty mind.

Doubt that the stars are fire; doubt that the sun doth move; doubt truth to be a liar; but never doubt I love.

O Romeo, Romeo, wherefore art thou Romeo?

*E*very man has business and desire, such as it is.

*T*o know the cause why music was ordain'd! Was it not to refresh the mind of a man after his studies or his usual pain?

*M*y library was dukedom large enough.

I pray thee cease thy counsel, which falls into mine ears as profitless as water in a sieve.

There's no art to find the mind's construction
in the face.

If they love they know not why, they hate upon no
better ground, they hate upon no better a ground.

My thoughts are whirled like a potter's wheel.

Their understanding begins to swell and the
approaching tide will shortly fill the reasonable
shores that now lie foul and muddy.

Your hearts are mighty, your skins are whole.

I am not only witty in myself, but the cause that wit is in other men.

This fell sergeant, death, is strict in his arrest.

Such as we are made of, such we be.

When we are born we cry that we are come to this great stage of fools.

Words, words, mere words, no matter from the heart.

The soul of this man is in his clothes.

He does it with better grace, but I do it more natural.

The play's the thing wherein I'll catch the conscience of the king.

Mine honour is my life; both grow in one; take honour from me and my life is done.

O Lord that lends me life, lend me a heart replete with thankfulness.

To be slow in words is a woman's only virtue.

O for a falconer's voice to lure this tassel-gentle back again.

How my achievements mock me!

Oft expectation fails, and most oft there where most it promises; and oft it hits where hope is coldest, and despair most fits.

Sweets to the sweet. Farewell.

Alas, their love may be call'd appetite. No motion of the liver, but the palate.

Small cheer and great welcome makes a merry feast.

Some cupid kills with arrows, some with traps.

Be thou as chaste as ice, as pure as snow, thou shalt not escape calumny. Get thee to a nunnery, go.

Golden lads and girls all must, as chimney-sweepers come to dust.

Imperious Caesar, dead and turn'd to clay, Might stop
a hole to keep the wind away.

We were not born to sue, but to command.

Pleasure and action make the hours seem short.

My ventures are not in one bottom trusted,
nor to one place.

Well, if Fortune be a woman, she's a good wench for this
gear.

In the spring time, the only pretty ring time, when birds do sing . . . sweet lovers love the spring.

Men shut their doors against a setting sun.

There's daggers in men's smiles.

If thou didst ever hold me in thy heart, absent thee from felicity awhile.

O, it came o'er my ear like the sweet sound that breathes upon a bank of violets, stealing and giving odour!

Merrily, merrily shall I live now, under the blossom that hangs on the bough.

But the strong base and building of my love is as the very centre of the earth, drawing all things to it.

Things done well and with a care, exempt themselves from fear.

Well-apparell'd April on the heel of limping winter treads.

An overflow of good converts to bad.

Thou art all the comfort the gods will diet me with.

Our bodies are our gardens to which our wills
are gardeners.

Things won are done, joy's soul lies in the doing.

For 'tis the sport to have the engineer hoist with his own
petard.

The robbed that smiles, steals something from the thief.

$\mathcal{G}$ive me that man that is not passion's
slave, and I will wear him in
my heart's core.

Lord, what fools these mortals be!

Pride, pomp, and circumstance of glorious war!

There are more things in heaven and earth, Horatio,
than are dreamt of in your philosophy

Some are born great, some achieve greatness, and some
have greatness thrust upon them.

I met a fool i' the forest, a motley fool.

A man I am cross'd with adversity.

Not that I loved Caesar less, but that I loved Rome more.

Adieu! I have too grieved a heart to take a tedious leave.

Tempt not a desperate man.

Love sought is good, but given unsought, is better.

The undiscover'd country from whose bourn no traveller returns, puzzles the will.

Short time seems long in sorrow's sharp sustaining.

To the last syllable of recorded time, and all our yesterdays have lighted fools the way to dusty death.

Truly, I would not hang a dog by my will, much more a man who hath any honesty in him.

Those scraps are good deeds past, which are devour'd as fast as they are made, forgot as soon as done.

*H*ere will be an old abusing of God's patience and the king's English.

*T*hey breathe truth that breathe their words in pain.

*M*en's evil manners live in brass; their virtues we write in water.

*W*e came into the world like brother and brother; and now let's go hand in hand, not one before another.

*T*he worst is not so long as we can say, this is the worst.

Now see that noble and most sovereign reason like sweet bells jangled out of tune and harsh.

There is nothing either good or bad but thinking makes it so.

Shake off this downy sleep, death's counterfeit, and look on death itself.

Love is a smoke made with the fume of sighs.

My age is as a lusty winter; frosty, but kindly.

A man in all the world's new fashion planted, that hath a mint of phrases in his brain.

My pride fell with my fortunes.

I hold the world but as the world, Gratiano;
a stage where every man must play a part,
and mine is a sad one.

A minist'ring angel shall my sister be when thou liest howling.

Parting is such sweet sorrow.

But love is blind and lovers cannot see the pretty follies that themselves commit.

Look on beauty, and you shall see 'tis purchased by the weight.

I bear a charmed life.

This is the excellent foppery of the world, that when we are sick in . . . we make guilty of our disasters the sun, the moon, and stars.

The cuckoo then on every tree mocks married men; for thus sings he: "Cuckoo!"

Friends, Romans, countrymen, lend me your ears; I
come to bury Caesar, not to praise him.

What a piece of work is a man!

Speak to me as to thy thinkings, as thou dost ruminate,
and give thy worst of thoughts the worst of words.

When we are married and have more occasion
to know one another: I hope, upon familiarity
will grow more contempt.

Fortune, that arrant whore, ne'er turns the key
to the poor.

There's not a note of mine that's worth the noting.

Come unto these yellow sands, And then take hands: courtsied when you have, and kiss'd the wild waves whist.

They do not love that do not show their love.

Pity is the virtue of the law, and none but tyrants use it cruelly.

Better three hours too soon than a minute too late.

If music be the food of love, play on, give me excess of it, that, surfeiting, the appetite may sicken, and so die.

Truth will come to light . . . at the length,
the truth will out.

Lady you bereft me of all words, only my blood speaks
to you in my veins, and there is such confusion in
my powers.

We must not make a scarecrow of the law, setting it up
to fear the birds of prey.

Love alters not with his brief hours and weeks, but
bears it out even to the edge of doom.

Love's best habit is a soothing tongue.

Cassius has a lean and hungry look; he thinks too much. Such men are dangerous.

Blow, blow, thou winter wind; thou art not so unkind as man's ingratitude.

The hand that hath made you fair hath made you good.

Assume a virtue, if you have it not.

Beauty itself doth of itself persuade the eyes of men without orator.

It will have blood, they say; blood will have blood.

Distribution should undo excess, and each man
    have enough.

Art thou not, fatal vision, sensible to feelings
    as to sight?

Speak the speech, I pray you, as I pronounced it to you,
    trippingly on the tongue.

To unpathed waters, undreamed shores.

We are advertis'd by our loving friends.

My tongue will tell the anger of mine heart, or else my heart, concealing it, will break.

His flight was madness: when our actions do not, our fears do make us traitors.

This above all; to thine own self be true.

They fool me to the top of my bent.

And many strokes, though with a little axe, hew down and fell the hardest-timbered oak.

I feel within me a peace above all earthly dignities, a still and quiet conscience.

Therefore all hearts in love use their own tongues; let every eye negotiate for itself and trust no agent.

Talkers are no good doers; be assur'd we come to use our hands and not our tongues.

How comes it, that thou art then estranged from thyself?

I wish you well and so I take my leave; I pray you know me when we meet again.

Patch grief with proverbs; make misfortune drunk.

Cursed be he that moves my bones.

Fair flowers that are not gather'd in their prime rot and consume themselves in little time.

Purpose is but the slave to memory, of violent birth, but poor validity.

And he that is more than a youth is not for me; and he that is less than a man, I am not for him.

The devil can cite Scripture for his purpose.

Fishes live in the sea, as men do a-land; the great ones eat up the little ones.

Come not within the measure of my wrath.

Talk'st thou to me of ifs! Thou art a traitor: off with his head!

There's a divinity that shapes our ends, rough-hew them how we will.

Bid suspicion double-lock the door.

The jury, passing on the prisoner's life, may in the sworn twelve have a thief or two guiltier than him they try.

This is a way to kill a wife with kindness.

Strong reasons make strong actions.

Music, moody food of us that trade in love.

To do a great right do a little wrong.

Much ado about nothing.

O Julius Caesar, thou art mighty yet. Thy spirit walks abroad and turns our swords in our own proper entrails.

Patience is sottish, and impatience does become a dog that's mad.

*H*e wears his faith but as
the fashion of his hat.

Under the greenwood tree who loves to lie
with me . . . Here shall he see no enemy
but winter and rough weather.

O what a rogue and peasant slave am I!

My heart suspects more than mine eye can see.

How poor are they that have not patience! What wound
did ever heal but by degrees?

His life was gentle, and the elements so mix'd in him
that Nature might stand up and say to all the world
"This was a man!"

And so from hour to hour, we ripe and ripe,
and then, from hour to hour, we rot and rot;
and thereby hangs a tale.

Nature hath framed strange fellows in her time.

What is the city but the people?

Out of this nettle, danger, we pluck this flower, safety.

When a father gives to his son, both laugh; when a son
gives to his father, both cry.

Art thou but a dagger of the mind, a false creation, proceeding from the heat-oppressed brain?

O thou invisible spirit of wine, if thou hast no name to be known by, let us call thee devil.

Thoughts are but dreams till their effects be tried.

Ambition should be made of sterner stuff.

Friendship is constant in all other things save in the office and affairs of love.

Maids are May when they are maids, but the sky changes when they are wives.

And in this harsh world draw thy breath in pain to tell my story.

Farewell! God knows when we shall meet again.

Heat not a furnace for your foe so hot that it do singe yourself.

Against my soul's pure truth, why labour you to make it wander in an unknown field?

This goodly frame the earth seems to me a sterile promontory, this most excellent canopy the air.

What is past is prologue.

That man that hath a tongue, I say, is no man, if with his tongue he cannot win a woman.

Best safety lies in fear.

He will give the devil his due.

This thought is as a death, which cannot choose but weep to have that which it fears to lose.

No legacy is so rich as honesty.

Give every man thy ear, but few thy voice; take each man's censure, but reserve thy judgment.

Thou art thy mother's glass, and she in thee calls back the lovely April of her prime.

The man that hath no music in himself, nor is not moved with concord of sweet sounds, is fit for treasons, stratagems, and spoils.

*H*ow many ages hence shall this our lofty scene be acted over in states unborn and accents yet unknown!

*B*y that sin fell the angels.

*F*etter strong madness in a silken thread.

*T*he purest treasure mortal times afford is spotless reputation; that away, men are but gilded loam or painted clay.

*I*t is a familiar beast to man, and signifies love.

In the night, imagining some fear, how easy is a bush
    suppos'd a bear!

I would forget it fain; but, O, it presses to my memory,
    like damned guilty deeds to a sinner's mind.

A man may fish with the worm that hath eat of a king,
    and eat of the fish that hath fed of that worm.

Seeing that death, a necessary end, will come when it
    will come.

When words are scarce they are seldom spent in vain.

The day shall not be up so soon as I, to
try the fair adventure of tomorrow.

I wasted time, and now doth time waste me.

*N*ow cracks a noble heart. Good night sweet prince:
and flights of angels sing thee to thy rest!

*S*o every bondman in his own hand bears the power
to cancel his captivity.

*T*here is no vice so simple but assumes some mark
of virtue on his outward parts.

*L*et Hercules himself do what he may, the cat will mew,
and dog will have his day.

*I*s it sin to rush into the secret house of death, ere death dare come to us?

*T*he fortune of us that are the moon's men doth ebb and flow like the sea, being governed, as the sea is, by the moon.

*I*f it were done, when 'tis done, then 'twere well it were done quickly.

*T*he quality of mercy is not strain'd, it droppeth as the gentle rain from heaven upon the place beneath.

*Y*ou cram these words into mine ears against the stomach of my sense.

God bless thee; and put meekness in thy mind, love, charity, obedience, and true duty!

As many arrows, loosed several ways, come to one mark . . . so may a thousand actions, once afoot, end in one purpose.

I am not merry; but I do beguile the thing I am, by seeming otherwise.

Hand in hand, with fairy grace, will we sing, and bless this place.

That love is merchandised whose rich esteeming the owner's tongue doth publish everywhere.

Excellent wretch! Perdition catch my soul, but I do love thee! And when I love thee not, chaos is come again.

As soon go kindle fire with snow, as seek to quench the fire of love with words.

'Tis neither here nor there.

The extreme parts of time extremely forms all causes to the purpose of his speed.

I see that the fashion wears out more apparel than the man.

How sharper than a serpent's tooth it is to have a thankless child!

Action is eloquence.

For 'tis a question left us yet to prove, whether love lead fortune, or else fortune love.

The instruments of darkness tell us truths, win us with honest trifles, to betray us in deepest consequence.

Care keeps his watch in every old man's eye, and where care lodges, sleep will never lie.

We know what we are, but know not what we may be.

Men are April when they woo, December when they wed.

Was ever book containing such vile matter so fairly bound? O, that deceit should dwell in such a gorgeous palace!

Ingratitude is monstrous, and for the multitude to be ungrateful, were to make a monster of the multitude.

Be not afraid of greatness.

Some rise by sin, and some by virtue fall.

What's mine is yours, and what is yours is mine.

So we grew together like to a double cherry, seeming parted, but yet an union in partition, two lovely berries moulded on one stem.

For in that sleep of death what dreams may come, when we have shuffled off this mortal coil.

O, she will sing the savageness out of a bear!

The ostentation of our love, which, left unshown, is often left unloved.

We are such stuff as dreams are made on; and our little life is rounded with a sleep.

Nature does require her times of preservation.

It is the stars, the stars above us, govern our conditions.

Not all the water in the rough rude sea can wash the balm off from an anointed king.

A stirring dwarf we do allowance give before
a sleeping giant.

*H*e who has injured thee was either stronger or
weaker than thee. If weaker, spare him; if stronger,
spare thyself.

I know myself now; and I feel within me a peace above
all earthly dignities, a still and quiet conscience.

I have a man's mind, but a woman's might.

*T*here lives within the very flame of love a kind of wick
or snuff that will abate it.

He jests at scars that never felt a wound. But soft, what light through yonder window breaks? It is the east and Juliet is the sun!

What's gone and what's past help should be past grief.

O God, I could be bounded in a nutshell and count myself a king of infinite space—were it not that I have bad dreams.

The poor beetle, that we tread upon, in corporal sufferance feels a pang as great as when a giant dies.

'Tis one thing to be tempted, another thing to fall.

*C*onscience does make cowards
of us all, and thus the native
hue of resolution is sicklied o'er
with the pale cast of thought.

It is the very error of the moon: she comes more nearer earth than she was wont, and makes men mad.

How sour sweet music is when time is broke and no proportion kept! So is it in the music of men's lives.

The very substance of the ambitious is merely the shadow of a dream.

Boldness be my friend.

There's such divinity doth hedge a king that treason can but peep to what it would.

Foolery does walk about the orb like the sun;
it shines everywhere.

To be, or not to be: that is the question.

O, beware, my lord, of jealousy! It is the green-eyed
monster which doth mock the meat it feeds on.

If love be blind, love cannot hit the mark.

Thus the whirligig of time brings in his revenges.

The sands are number'd that make up my life.

This fellow pecks up wit, as pigeons peas; and utters it again when God doth please: he is wit's peddler; and retails his wares.

When beggars die, there are no comets seen; the heavens themselves blaze forth the death of princes.

The time is out of joint: O cursed spite, that ever I was born to set it right!

Our revels now are ended. These our actors, as I foretold you, were all spirits, and are melted into air, into thin air.

Present fears are less than horrible imaginings.

Ask me no reason why I love you; for though
Love use Reason for his physician, he admits
him not for his counsellor.

O pardon me, thou bleeding piece of earth, that
I am meek and gentle with these butchers.

A fool thinks himself to be wise, but a wise man knows
himself to be a fool.

My love admits no qualifying dross.

Our doubts are traitors and make us lose the good we oft might win by fearing to attempt.

But 'tis strange and oftentimes, to win us to our harm, the instruments of darkness tell us truths.

Love looks not with the eyes, but with the mind; and therefore is winged Cupid painted blind.

For there was never yet philosopher that could endure the toothache patiently.

The common curse of mankind—folly and ignorance.

Time's glory is to command contending kings, to unmask falsehood, and bring truth to light.

That we should, with joy, pleasance, revel, and applause, transform ourselves into beasts!

He that has a house to put his head in has a good head-piece.

To thine own self be true, and it must follow, as the night the day, thou canst not then be false to any man.

But if the while I think on thee, dear friend, all losses are restored and sorrows end.

I have heard of your paintings well enough. God hath
    given you one face and you make yourselves another.

He then unto the ladder turns his back, looks
    in the clouds, scorning the base degrees
    by which he did ascend.

Time is like a fashionable host that slightly shakes his
    parting guest by the hand.

But music for the time doth change his nature.

Fill all thy bones with aches.

Leave her to heaven and to those thorns that in her bosom lodge, to prick and sting her.

To gild refined gold, to paint the lily . . . is wasteful and ridiculous excess.

Love is too young to know what conscience is.

Uneasy lies the head that wears a crown.

Matter and impertinency mix'd! Reason in madness!

$\mathcal{B}$etter a witty fool than a foolish wit.

You would pluck out the heart of my mystery.

Though thou speak'st truth, methink thou
speak'st not well.

Lord, Lord, how subject we old men are
to this vice of lying!

There is a tide in the affairs of men, which taken
at the flood, leads on to fortune.

The evil that men do lives after them; the good is oft
interred with their bones.

*M*en were deceivers ever—one foot in the sea and one on shore, to one thing constant never.

*H*e that is giddy thinks the world turns round.

*I*t is not in the stars to hold our destiny but in ourselves; we are underlings.

*H*e takes false shadows for true substances.

O, she is rich in beauty, only poor that, when she dies, with beauty dies her store.

Ruin has taught me to ruminate, that time will come and take my love away.

Belike you thought our love would last too long, if it were chain'd together.

He that is robb'd, not wanting what is stolen, let him not know 't, and he's not robb'd at all.

Trust not him that has once broken faith.

Condemn the fault, and not the actor of it?

As the last taste of sweets, is sweetest last, writ in remembrance more than things long past.

This thou perceivest, which makes thy love more strong, to love that well which thou must leave ere long.

Give sorrow words; the grief that does not speak whispers the o'er-fraught heart and bids it break.

O sleep, O gentle sleep, nature's soft nurse, how have I frighted thee

The law hath not been dead, though it hath slept.

Sleep, that sometimes shuts up sorrow's eye, steal me
awhile from mine own company.

Women being the weaker vessels, are ever thrust
to the walls.

Canst thou not minister to a mind diseased, pluck from
the memory a rooted sorrow?

A very little thief of occasion will rob you of a great
deal of patience.

No profit grows where is no pleasure ta'en; in brief, sir,
study what you most affect.

Ignorance is the curse of God; knowledge is the wing wherewith we fly to heaven.

The gaudy, blabbing, and remorseful day is crept into the bosom of the sea.

It easeth some, though none it ever cured, to think their dolour others have endured.

Talking isn't doing. It is a kind of good deed to say well; and yet words are not deeds.

It seems she hangs upon the cheek of night as a rich jewel in an Ethiop's ear—beauty too rich for use, for earth too dear.

Where love is great, the littlest doubts are fear; where little fear grows great, great love grows there.

If love be blind, it best agrees with night.

'Tis in ourselves that we are thus or thus. Our bodies are our gardens to which our wills are gardeners.

I am a man more sinn'd against than sinning.

O, what a goodly outside falsehood hath!

The glass of fashion and the mould of form.

Let me not to the marriage of true minds admit impediments: love is not love which alters when it alteration finds.

I can no other answer make, but, thanks, and thanks.

A little more than kin, and less than kind.

We may outrun by violent swiftness and lose by over-running.

Something is rotten in the state of Denmark.

Were such things here as we do speak about?
Or have we eaten on the insane root that takes
the reason prisoner?

But men are men, the best sometimes forget.

Vows were ever brokers to defiling.

The wheel is come full circle.

I was adored once, too.

*O*ur peace shall stand as firm as rocky mountains.

*I*s it not strange that desire should so many years outlive performance?

*T*here is no virtue like necessity.

*T*he innocent sleep, sleep that knits up the raveled sleeve of care . . .

*F*rame your mind to mirth and
merriment, which bars a thousand
harms and lengthens life.

*M*an delights not me—nor woman neither, though by your smiling you seem to say so.

*W*hen to the sessions of sweet silent thought I summon up remembrance of things past, I sigh.

*B*ut where unbruised youth with unstuff'd brain doth couch his limbs, there golden sleep doth reign.

*I*f that the world and love were young, and truth in every shepherd's tongue.

*W*omen speak two languages—one of which is verbal.

Cowards die many times before their deaths; the valiant never taste of death but once.

Virtue is bold, and goodness never fearful.

Past and to come, seems best; things present, worse.

Modest doubt is called the beacon of the wise.

A grandma's name is little less in love than is the doting title of a mother.

I am sure care's an enemy to life.

*N*o, 'tis not so deep as a well, nor so wide as a church door, but 'tis enough, 'twill serve.

*W*hat is love? 'Tis not hereafter, present mirth hath present laughter: what's to come is still unsure.

*T*here's nothing ill can dwell in such a temple: if the ill spirit have so fair a house, good things will strive to dwell with 't.

O judgment, thou art fled to brutish beasts and men have lost their reason.

He is well paid that is well satisfied.

Beauty is but a vain and doubtful good; a shining gloss
that fadeth suddenly; a flower that dies when first it
'gins to bud.

Kindness in women, not their beauteous looks,
shall win my love.

Though I want a kingdom, yet in marriage I may not
prove inferior to yourself.

I never see thy face but I think upon hell-fire.

The miserable have no other medicine, but only hope.

Wishers were ever fools.

My crown is in my heart, not in my head, nor decked with diamonds and Indian stones, nor to be seen.

What is a man, if his chief good and market of his time be but to sleep and feed? A beast, no more.

Thou hast not youth nor age, but, as it were, an after-dinner's sleep, dreaming on both.

An honest tale speeds best, being plainly told.

Upon the heat and flame of thy distemper sprinkle cool patience.

How far that little candle throws its beams! So shines a good deed in a naughty world.

But he that filches from me my good name robs me of that which not enriches him and makes me poor indeed.

All deeds are doubled with an evil word.

*F*oul cankering rust the hidden treasure frets, but gold that's put to use more gold begets.

*B*y the pricking of my thumbs, something wicked this way comes. Open, locks, whoever knocks!

*I*f this were played upon a stage now, I could condemn it as an improbable fiction.

*M*en have marble—women, waxen—minds.

*M*en of few words are the best men.

Life every man holds dear; but the dear man holds honor far more precious dear than life.

Brevity is the soul of wit.

Reputation is an idle and most false imposition; oft got without merit, and lost without deserving.

When he is best, he is a little worse than a man; and when he is worst, he is little better than a beast.

Let me embrace thee, sour adversity, for wise men say it is the wisest course.

The valiant never taste of death but once.

The fringed curtains of thine eye advance.

We do not keep the outward form of order, where there is deep disorder in the mind.

Do not banish reason for inequality; but let your reason serve to make the truth appear where it seems hid.

It is a good divine that follows his own instructions.

Praising what is lost makes the remembrance dear.

Hereafter, in a better world than this, I shall desire more love and knowledge of you.

See what a ready tongue suspicion hath!

Confusion now hath made his masterpiece.

So full of artless jealousy is guilt, it spills itself in fearing to be spilt.

Tomorrow, and tomorrow, and tomorrow, creeps in this petty pace from day to day.

Love's not time's fool, though rosy lips and cheeks
within his bending sickle's compass come.

Against self-slaughter there is a prohibition so divine
that cravens my weak hand.

Praise us as we are tasted, allow us as we prove.

Now let it work. Mischief, thou art afoot: take thou
what course thou wilt.

Though fortunes malice overthrow my state, my mind
exceeds the compass of her wheel.

Speak low, if you speak love.

This is the third time; I hope good luck lies in odd numbers . . . There is divinity in odd numbers, either in nativity, chance, or death.

Suit the action to the word, the word to the action.

A great perturbation in nature, to receive at once the benefit of sleep and do the effects of watching!

It is a wise father that knows his own child.

Small to greater matters must give way.

A peace is of the nature of a conquest; for then both parties nobly are subdued, and neither party loser.

The best in this kind are but shadows.

Have more than thou showest; speak less than thou knowest.

He must needs go that the devil drives.

With mirth and laughter let old wrinkles come.

True is it that we have seen better days.

Come, gentlemen, I hope we shall drink down all unkindness.

The better part of valor is discretion, in the which better part I have saved my life.

Who could refrain that had a heart to love and in that heart courage to make love known?

A heavy heart bears not a nimble tongue.

I thank God I am as honest as any man living that is an old man and no more honest than I.

'Twas never merry world since lowly feigning was called compliment.

Most dangerous is that temptation that doth goad us on to sin in loving virtue.

Those that she makes fair she scarce makes honest; and those that she makes honest she makes very ill-favouredly.

Rich gifts wax poor when givers prove unkind.

Though men can cover crimes with bold stern looks,
poor women's faces are their own faults' books.

I do not speak to thee in drink but in tears, not in
pleasure but in passion, not in words only, but in
woes also.

There is a devilish mercy in the judge, if you'll implore
it, that will free your life, but fetter you till death.

How well he's read, to reason against reading!

I like not fair terms and a villain's mind.

This England never did, nor never shall, lie at the proud foot of a conqueror.

O what may man within him hide, though angel on the outward side!

Desire of having is the sin of covetousness.

Women may fall when there's no strength in men.

The love of heaven makes one heavenly.

Why, this is very midsummer madness.

I do oppose my patience to his fury, and am arm'd
to suffer with a quietness of spirit, the very tyranny
and rage of his.

This bud of love, by summer's ripening breath, may
prove a beauteous flower when next we meet.

What power is it which mounts my love so high, that
makes me see, and cannot feed mine eye?

*P*oor and content is rich,
and rich enough.

Give thy thoughts no tongue.

Life is as tedious as twice-told tale, vexing the dull ear
of a drowsy man.

Mercy is not itself, that oft looks so.

Thieves for their robbery have authority when judges
steal themselves.

I love you with so much of my heart that none is left
to protest.

Sweet flowers are slow and weeds make haste.

Now is the winter of our discontent.

I say there is no darkness but ignorance.

Neither a borrower nor a lender be; for loan oft loses
both itself and friend, and borrowing dulls the edge
of husbandry.

There was never yet fair woman but she made mouths
in a glass.

Having nothing, nothing can he lose.

'Tis better to bear the ills we have than fly to others that we know not of.

What, man, defy the devil. Consider, he's an enemy to mankind.

This world is not for aye, nor 'tis not strange that even our loves should with our fortunes change.

She is mine own, and I as rich in having such a jewel as twenty seas . . . The water nectar, and the rocks pure gold.

Frailty, thy name is woman!

He that sleeps feels not the tooth-ache.

The gods are just, and of our pleasant vices make instruments to plague us.

I am the very pink of courtesy.

Beware the ides of March.

While thou livest keep a good tongue in thy head.

Nothing 'gainst Time's scythe can make defense.

Throw physic to the dogs; I'll none of it.

Now, God be praised, that to believing souls gives light in darkness, comfort in despair.

Good night, good night! Parting is such sweet sorrow, that I shall say good night till it be morrow.

Few love to hear the sins they love to act.

One touch of nature makes the whole world kin.

Men's vows are women's traitors!

But wonder on, till truth makes all things plain.

The hind that would be mated by the lion must
die for love.

A jest's prosperity lies in the ear of him that hears it,
never in the tongue of him that makes it.

There is special providence in the fall of a sparrow.

I have no spur to prick the sides of my intent, but only vaulting ambition, which o'erleaps itself, and falls on the other.

W here every something, being blent together turns to a wild of nothing.

S wear not by the moon, th' inconstant moon, that monthly changes in her circled orb, lest that thy love prove likewise variable.

I have sworn thee fair, and thought thee bright, who art as black as hell, as dark as night.

B e check'd for silence, but never tax'd for speech.

I did never know so full a voice issue from so empty a heart: but the saying is true, "The empty vessel makes the greatest sound."

Self-love, my liege, is not so vile a sin as self-neglecting.

Within the hollow crown That rounds the mortal temples of a king Keeps Death his court.

The golden age is before us, not behind us.

O, I am fortune's fool.

I understand a fury in your words,
but not the words.

All days are nights to see till I see thee, and nights bright days when dreams do show thee to me.

Love surfeits not, Lust like a glutton dies; Love is all truth, Lust full of forged lies.

I hold ambition of so light a quality that is but a shadow's shadow.

Nothing emboldens sin so much as mercy.

A man loves the meat in his youth that he cannot endure in his age.

What a deformed thief this fashion is.

The trust I have is in mine innocence, and therefore am
I bold and resolute.

But screw your courage to the sticking-place,
and we'll not fail.

And this, our life, exempt from public haunt, finds . . .
good in everything.

Now would I give a thousand furlongs of sea for an acre
of barren ground.

Weighest thy words before thou givest them breath.

O God! God! How weary, stale, flat, and unprofitable
seem to me all the uses of this world!

The poet's eye, in a fine frenzy rolling, doth glance from
heaven to earth, from earth to heaven.

What's in a name? That which we call a rose by any
other name would smell as sweet.

In a false quarrel there is no true valor.

Double, double toil and trouble; fire burn, and
cauldron bubble.

Everyone ought to bear patiently the results
of his own conduct.

There's some ill planet reigns: I must be patient till the
heavens look with an aspect more favourable.

If wishes would prevail with me, my purpose should not
fail with me.

The old folk: time's doting chronicles.

*N*o, I will be the pattern of all patience;
I will say nothing.

*T*hen must you speak of one that loved not wisely
but too well.

*I*n sweet music is such art: killing care and grief of heart
fall asleep, or hearing, die.

I were better to be eaten to death with a rust than to be
scoured to nothing with perpetual motion.

*T*here is no fettering of authority.

Things sweet to taste prove in digestion sour.

Maids want nothing but husbands, and when they have them, they want everything.

There's beggary in the love that can be reckon'd.

I will fasten on this sleeve of thine: thou art an elm, my husband, I a vine.

The expedition of my violent love outrun the pauser, reason.

A merry heart goes all the day; your sad tires in a mile.

Your face, my thane, is as a book where men may read strange matters.

They are as sick that surfeit with too much, as they starve with nothing.

Have you not heard it said full oft, a woman's nay doth stand for naught.

Sweetest things turn sourest by their deeds; lilies that fester smell far worse than weeds.

*T*hough I am not naturally honest, I am so sometimes
by chance.

*I*t is not, nor it cannot come to good. But break, my
heart, for I must hold my tongue.

*L*et every eye negotiate for itself and trust no agent.

*T*ime's the king of men; he's both their parent, and he
is their grave, and gives them what he will, not what
they crave.

*T*he web of our life is of a mingled yarn,
good and ill together.

Love is begun by time; and that I see in passages of proof, time qualifies the spark and fire of it.

A high hope for a low heaven: God grant us patience!

Death is a fearful thing.

A woman impudent and mannish grown is not more loathed than an effeminate man in time of action.

Every why hath a wherefore.

*A*ge cannot wither her, nor custom stale
her infinite variety.

O fortune, fortune! All men call thee fickle.

*G*od has given you one face, and you make
yourself another.

*D*o you not know I am a woman? When I think,
I must speak.

*O*h! That you could turn your eyes towards the napes of
your necks, and make but an interior survey of your
good selves.

Make not your thoughts your prisons.

False face must hide what the false heart doth know.

He that hath a beard is more than a youth, and he that hath no beard is less than a man.

For I can raise no money by vile means.

Like as the waves make towards the pebbl'd shore, so do our minutes, hasten to their end.

Sweet are the uses of adversity which, like the toad, ugly and venomous, wears yet a precious jewel in his head.

To weep is to make less the depth of grief.

Winter, which, being full of care, makes summer's welcome thrice more wish'd, more rare.

But thought's the slave of life, and life time's fool.

Home-keeping youth have ever homely wits.

He that loves to be flattered is worthy o' the flatterer.

The course of true love never did run smooth.
Love is a familiar. Love is a devil. There is
no evil angel but Love.

For my part, it was Greek to me.

Silence is the perfectest herald of joy: I were but little
happy, if I could say how much.

What's done can't be undone.

Well, I will find you twenty lascivious turtles ere one
chaste man.

'Tis better to be lowly born, and range with humble livers in content, than to be perked up in a glistering grief, and wear a golden sorrow.

Misery acquaints a man with strange bedfellows.

Love thrives not in the heart that shadows dreadeth.

He draweth out the thread of his verbosity finer than the staple of his argument.

Young in limbs, in judgment old.

'Tis not enough to help the feeble up, but to support them after.

Adversity's sweet milk, philosophy.

Many that are not mad have, sure, more lack of reason.

As flies to wanton boys, are we to the gods; they kill us for their sport.

The attempt and not the deed confounds us.

And oftentimes excusing of a fault doth make the fault the worse by the excuse.

I had rather have a fool to make me merry than experience to make me sad and to travel for it, too!

Is love a tender thing? It is too rough, too rude, too boist'rous, and it pricks like a thorn.

And ruin'd love when it is built anew, grows fairer than at first, more strong, far greater.

Time hath a wallet at his back wherein he puts alms for oblivion, a great-sized monster of ingratitudes.

*B*ut miserable most, to love unloved? This you should pity rather than despise.

*F*aith, there hath been many great men that have flattered the people who ne'er loved them.

*W*e have some salt of our youth in us.

O curse of marriage, that we can call these delicate creatures ours, and not their appetites.

*W*hen sorrows come, they come not single spies, but in battalions.

Life's but a walking shadow, a poor player, that struts and frets his hour upon the stage.

Though this be madness, yet there is method in 't.

Out, damned spot! Out, I say!

The whirligig of time brings in his revenges.

Many a good hanging prevents a bad marriage.

*M*ind your speech a little lest you
should mar your fortunes.

Ah, what a sign it is of evil life, where death's approach is seen so terrible!

O that a man might know the end of this day's business ere it come!

Children wish fathers looked but with their eyes; fathers that children with their judgment looked; and either may be wrong.

If you have tears, prepare to shed them now.

He's loved of the distracted multitude, who like not in their judgment, but their eyes.

The moon's an errant thief, and her pale fire she snatches from the sun.

O how full of briers is this working-day world!

O, had I but followed the arts!

Love all, trust a few, do wrong to none.

Madness in great ones must not unwatch'd go.

Time and the hour run through the roughest day.

Let me not live, after my flame lacks oil, to be the snuff
of younger spirits.

Fortune brings in some boats that are not steered.

When valour preys on reason,
it eats the sword it fights with.

An old man is twice a child.

Every man has his fault, and honesty is his.

Our remedies oft in ourselves do lie.

*A*nd what have kings that privates have not too, save ceremony, save general ceremony?

*N*or do not saw the air too much with your hand, thus, but use all gently.

*L*ove to faults is always blind, always is to joy inclined. Lawless, winged, and unconfined, and breaks all chains from every mind.

A thought which, quarter'd, hath but one part wisdom and ever three parts coward.

*I*f it be a sin to covet honor, I am the most offending soul.

I have no other but a woman's reason: I think him so, because I think him so.

The end crowns all, and that old common arbitrator, Time, will one day end it.

If all the year were playing holidays, to sport would be as tedious as to work.

I am as vigilant as a cat to steal cream.

'Tis beauty that doth oft make women proud.

My love is strengthen'd, though more weak in seeming; I love not less, though less the show appear.

O, how this spring of love resembleth the uncertain glory of an April day!

Sorrow concealed, like an oven stopp'd, doth burn the heart to cinders where it is.

He is winding the watch of his wit; by and by it will strike.

My words fly up, my thoughts remain below. Words without thoughts never to heaven go.

When love begins to sicken and decay, it useth an enforced ceremony.

If we are marked to die, we are enough to do our country loss; and if to live, the fewer men, the greater share of honor.

The lady doth protest too much, methinks.

How hard it is for women to keep counsel!

Mercy but murders, pardoning those that kill.

*B*ut I am constant as the northern star, of whose true-fixed and resting quality there is no fellow in the firmament.

*C*all home thy ancient thoughts from banishment.

*H*e that wants money, means, and content is without three good friends.

*T*he chameleon Love can feed on the air.

*O*ne may smile, and smile, and be a villain.

For this the foolish over-careful fathers have broke their sleep with thoughts, their brains with care, their bones with industry.

Oh, I have lost my reputation! I have lost the immortal part of myself, and what remains is bestial.

I am not bound to please thee with my answer.

Things base and vile, holding no quantity, love can transpose to form and dignity.

You shall more command with years than with your weapons.

Who steals my purse steals trash.

The peace of heaven is theirs that lift their swords,
in such a just and charitable war.

[Marriage is] a world-without-end bargain.

If you prick us do we not bleed? If you tickle us do we
not laugh? If you poison us do we not die? If you
wrong us shall we not revenge?

Care I for the limb, the thews, the stature, bulk, and
big assemblance of a man! Give me the spirit.

Why, then the world's mine oyster,
which I with sword will open.

If there were reason for these miseries, then into limits could I bind my woes.

They say miracles are past.

Shall I compare thee to a summer's day? Thou art more lovely and more temperate.

Be it art or hap, he hath spoken true.

'Tis best to weigh the enemy more mighty than he seems.

There is left us ourselves to end ourselves.

O God, O God, how weary, stale, flat, and unprofitable seem to me all the uses of this world!

Love's reason's without reason.

Though patience be a tired mare, yet she will plod.

He hath eaten me out of house and home.

I will praise any man that will praise me.

Hell is empty and all the devils are here.

True hope is swift, and flies with swallow's wings;
kings it makes gods, and meaner creatures kings.

O God, that men should put an enemy in their mouths to
steal away their brains!

Thou shalt be both the plaintiff and the judge of thine
own cause.

For we, which now behold these present days, have eyes
to wonder, but lack tongues to praise.

Thou art not for the fashion of these times, where none
will sweat but for promotion.

We are not ourselves when nature, being oppress'd, commands the mind to suffer with the body.

Things are often spoke and seldom meant.

Therefore, since brevity is the soul of wit, and tediousness the limbs and outward flourishes, I will be brief.

Ornament is but the guiled shore to a most dangerous sea.

Do not swear at all. Or if thou wilt, swear by thy gracious self, which is the god of my idolatry.

*B*ut yesterday the word of Caesar might have stood against the world. Now lies he there, and none so poor to do him reverence.

*I*n idle wishes fools supinely stay; be there a will, then wisdom finds a way.

*O*ut, out, brief candle! Life's but a walking shadow, a poor player that struts and frets his hour upon the stage.

*A*s he was valiant, I honor him: but as he was ambitious, I slew him.

*T*he stroke of death is as a lover's pinch, which hurts and is desired.

Men at some time are the masters of their fates: the fault, dear Brutus, is not in our stars, but in ourselves, that we are underlings.

But look, the morn in russet mantle clad walks o'er the dew of yon high eastward hill.

You and I are past our dancing days.

He was a man, take him for all in all, I shall not look upon his like again.

The sweetest honey is loathsome in his own deliciousness and in the taste confounds the appetite.

*Y*et do I fear thy nature; it is too full o' the milk of human kindness.

*I*n time we hate that which we often fear.

*T*o fear the foe, since fear oppresseth strength, gives in your weakness strength unto your foe.

*I*f you can look into the seeds of time, and say which grain will grow and which will not, speak then unto me.